Rookie Read-About® Science

Gentle Gorillas and Other Apes

By Allan Fowler

Consultants:
Robert L. Hillerich, Professor Emeritus,
Bowling Green State University, Bowling Green, Ohio
Consultant, Pinellas County Schools, Florida

Lynne Kepler, Educational Consultant

Fay Robinson, Child Development Specialist

CHILDRENS PRESS®
CHICAGO

Design by Beth Herman Design Associates

Library of Congress Cataloging-in-Publication Data

Fowler, Allan.
  Gentle gorillas and other apes / by Allan Fowler.
    p. cm. – (Rookie read-about science)
  ISBN 0-516-06022-8
  1. Apes–Juvenile literature. [1. Apes.] I. Title.
  II. Series: Fowler, Allan. Rookie read-about science.
QL737.P96F68   1994
599.88–dc20   93-38590
                                                        CIP
                                                         AC

This gorilla is beating on
his chest and making a
loud, hooting noise.

Is he about to attack?
No, he is simply scaring
intruders away.

Gorillas are very strong,
but they are also gentle.

Gorillas are apes – the largest apes of all.

Apes belong to a family of animals called primates.

Monkeys are also primates.

So are human beings.

All primates have fingers,
and many have thumbs.
They can hold onto things.

How can you tell an ape
from a monkey? If it has
a tail, it's not an ape.

Apes never have tails.
And apes are bigger
than monkeys.

A full-grown male gorilla
is about as tall as a man.

But a gorilla weighs two or
three times more than a man.

Though gorillas are able to stand, they walk on all fours.

They keep their hands
bent when they walk,
so their knuckles touch
the ground.

Try walking that way.
It's hard for you...but
easy for a gorilla, because
a gorilla's arms are much
longer than its legs.

Gorillas in the wild live in
groups called troops. An
older male, with silver hair
on his back, is the leader
of each troop.

To make sure gorillas do not die out, some of their homelands in Africa are now protected.

Besides gorillas, there
are three other kinds of
apes – chimpanzees,

orangutans, and gibbons.

Chimpanzees, like gorillas,
come from Africa and live
in troops.

They are smaller than
gorillas, but have
bigger ears.

Chimpanzees, or chimps, are the smartest of all the apes. They use twigs as tools to help them eat.

This chimp has even been taught to "talk" with people – by using sign language.

Orangutans, too, are very smart and can be taught things. Their hair is reddish-brown.

It's easy to tell the females and males apart. The males have big pouches of skin on their faces.

Orangutans live in
the forests of Borneo
and Sumatra.

Those are islands near
Southeast Asia.

Not far away, on the
Asian mainland, are the
forests where gibbons live.

Gibbons are the smallest apes.

They spend most of their time in trees.

Gibbons walk along the branches on their two legs – or swing from branch to branch, using their long, strong arms.

Chimps and orangutans
also swing through
the trees.

But you won't see adult
gorillas doing that.

They're so heavy that
they'd break the branches.

Words You Know

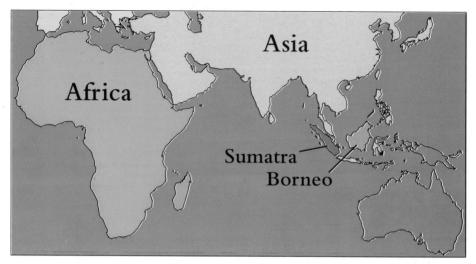

Apes are found in Africa, Asia, Sumatra, and Borneo.

gorilla

chimpanzee (chimp)

orangutan

gibbons

primate

monkey

troop

Index

About the Author

Allan Fowler is a free-lance writer with a background in advertising. Born in New York, he lives in Chicago now and enjoys traveling.

Photo Credits

Animals Animals – ©H.S. Terrace, 21

©Carl Purcell – 12

Tom Stack & Associates – ©Larry Tackett, 17 (left); ©Denise Tackett, 17 (right); ©Brian Parker, 23, 31 (top left)

SuperStock International, Inc. – 16; ©Alan Briere, Cover; ©Deborah Levinson, 7, 31 (center left); ©Roy King, 18, 19, 30 (bottom right); ©B. Amadeus Rubel, 22

Valan – ©Kennon Cooke, 5, 25, 26, 30 (bottom left), 31 (top right); ©John Cancalosi, 8, 29; ©James D. Markou, 9, 31 (center right); ©Robert C. Simpson, 11

Visuals Unlimited – ©Science VU, 3; ©Joe McDonald, 4; ©Walt Anderson, 15

The Wildlife Collection – ©Martin Harvey, 14, 31 (bottom); ©John Giustina, 20

Beth Herman Design Associates – map 30

COVER: Mountain Gorilla